STO

For Kate and Ellie,
Mirandas both... but better – CP

Text copyright © Chris Powling 2000
Illustrations copyright © Tony Morris 2000

Published in Great Britain in 2000
by Hodder Wayland, an imprint of
Hodder Children's Books

A catalogue record for this book is available from
the British Library.

ISBN: 0 7500 2996 X

Printed in Hong Kong by Wing King Tong

Hodder Children's Books
A division of Hodder Headline Limited
338 Euston Road, London NW1 3BH

The Shakespeare Collection

THE TEMPEST

RETOLD BY CHRIS POWLING

Illustrated by Tony Morris

H O D D E R
Wayland

an imprint of Hodder Children's Books

 *Character list:*

Prospero

Miranda
(Prospero's daughter)

Ariel
(Spirit)

Caliban
(Sycorax's son)

Ferdinand
(King Alonso's son)

Gonzalo
(Prospero's friend)

Alonso
(King)

Antonio
(Prospero's brother)

Sebastian
(King Alonso's brother)

Trinculo
(the king's jester)

Stephano
(the king's butler)

Long ago, on a faraway island, Prospero the magician was conjuring a storm. It was no ordinary storm, either. This was a full-scale tempest – a sea-quaking, sky-shaking catastrophe with thunder and lightning so close together that you couldn't tell the flash from the crash of it. And right in the eye of the storm, a ship was struggling to stay afloat.

Miranda, Prospero's daughter, was almost in tears. "Won't you stop it, father?" she begged. "That ship's being torn to pieces. Everyone on board will be drowned!"

"Or saved, perhaps," said Prospero.

Miranda stared at her father, bewildered. How could anyone be saved when the wind and the waves were so frantic and the sky so threatening?

Prospero took his daughter's hand. Now, at last, he could tell her why they'd settled in this remote place.

"Miranda," he said, gently. "We've lived here for twelve long years. You were a child of three when we arrived. Can you remember our life before that?"

"Only servants, father. Did I have four or five servants to look after me?"

"Many more, my dear," replied Prospero. "Once, you see, I was a great prince – the Duke of Milan, no less. And you were a princess."

"So what brought us here?" asked Miranda.

Horrified, she listened as her father told the whole story...

Prospero had been betrayed by his own
brother, Antonio. While Prospero was wrapped
up in his magic, Antonio was busy plotting to
raise an army with the help of Prospero's rival,
King Alonso of Naples. Together they took over
his dukedom.

Antonio didn't dare murder his brother openly. Instead, with his infant daughter in his arms, Prospero had been abandoned far out to sea in an ancient, worm-eaten rowing boat. They'd have both been lost but for the help of an honest friend called Gonzalo. Secretly, he'd fitted the boat with everything they needed to reach the island – including Prospero's precious magic books.

Miranda was amazed. "This Gonzalo saved our lives, father? What a lovely man! Where is he now, I wonder?"

"Out there," said Prospero.

"In the storm?" cried Miranda. "But he'll die! What has he done to deserve that?"

Prospero smiled grimly. When he spoke again there was so much pain in his voice that Miranda barely recognized it. "Gonzalo is not alone on that ship, Miranda," he said. "King Alonso is on board as well with his young son, Ferdinand. And so is the man who stole my throne..."

"Antonio, your brother?"

"My *treacherous* brother, Miranda."

Before his daughter could say another word, Prospero waved his wand. Miranda fell asleep at once.

*P*rospero and Miranda were not alone on the island.

Once, a wicked witch called Sycorax had lived there, and the place was as evil and as ugly as herself. After Sycorax died, Prospero had used his cloak and wand and spellbooks to transform a landscape of rock and brambles into a garden surrounded by the sea. He'd also released every spirit that Sycorax had kept prisoner – except for Ariel, the liveliest spirit of all.

"One day, you'll be free as well," the magician promised.

"Thank you, Master!" Ariel sang, as he glimmered this way and that in the air. "Until then, I'll be your eyes and ears all over the island – and your nose, too, so you can always sniff out trouble!"

Trouble? In a paradise as lovely as this?

*O*ne trouble came by the name of Caliban.
He was the witch's lazy monster of a son – a
snuffling, shuffling bundle of resentment with an
attitude even Prospero couldn't improve. Instead,
he kept Caliban as a servant, and set him to work
on the island.

"He's taught me how to talk," angry Caliban
would snarl. "So now I can curse him. And his
daughter, Miranda, too. This island belongs
to *me*!"

"You think so?" Ariel always asked.

"I know so."

"Then I'd better show you who's boss!"
And, gleefully, Ariel would pinch Caliban
back to work again...

$\mathcal{A}$riel had managed the tempest perfectly. Exactly as Prospero had ordered, he lit the ship from one end to the other with a ghostly glow even scarier than the storm itself. Using more magic, Ariel transported the ship and its crew to a secret cove, while the royal party were swept ashore and scattered all over the island.

Now they had to fend for themselves.

But only King Alonso's son, Prince Ferdinand, was completely alone. Confused and frightened, he staggered up the beach towards Prospero's cave, led on and on by Ariel's eerie singing:

"Full fathom five thy father lies;
  Of his bones are coral made..."

Ferdinand was in despair, certain that his father was dead. "Not just my father," he groaned. "Isn't everyone lost except me? Where am I, anyway? This place is so strange, so heavenly—"

Then, in the cave entrance, he saw Miranda.

Still half-asleep, Miranda gazed back at the handsome stranger – the first man she'd ever met apart from her father. "Who is he?" she whispered under her breath. "Is he some kind of god?"

"And are you some kind of goddess?" breathed Ferdinand, sinking to his knees. He'd never seen a woman so beautiful.

Prospero interrupted icily. "She's my daughter," he said. "And as human as I am. Have you come here to spy on us?"

"A spy, sir? I'm no spy—"

"And I'm no fool, young man. Miranda, we must make this castaway our prisoner. We'll lock him in chains and feed him on acorns and seawater, with hard labour to earn his keep – until we're certain that we can trust him."

"And how will you keep me prisoner, sir?" asked Ferdinand, reaching for his sword.

"Like this," replied Prospero. And instantly, as the magician lifted his wand, Ferdinand's weapon clattered from his hand.

Miranda stared at all this in dismay. Why was her father being so cruel? And what was he whispering to Ariel, his invisible helper? Were they following some kind of plan?

Elsewhere on the island, Caliban had a nasty plan of his own. He'd gained a pair of helpers as well, both survivors from the shipwreck – Stephano, the king's butler, and Trinculo, his jester. They'd managed to save some wine from the ship and were making the most of it.

"When all this is over," said Caliban with a burp, "Prospero will stink like a bog from every nastiness under the sun! That should pay him back for the way he's treated me!"

"How about paying *us* back for all the wine you've drunk, Big Gob?" said Stephano, snatching the bottle.

Trinculo nodded blearily. "That's right," he agreed. "From the moment we met, you've done nothing but guzzle our booze, Uglymug. Here, let me have a swig."

"Listen," belched the butler. "There's that strange music again! It's the spookiest sound I've ever heard."

"Don't be afraid," said Caliban. "This place is full of music. It's as normal as the sigh of the wind or the flop of the waves, like a ghostly orchestra that sets the whole island dreaming... and if you'll help me, it can all be yours!"

Trinculo couldn't believe it. "Our very own island?" he asked.

"All yours, my masters."

"And what must we do to earn it?"

Caliban smiled. Or maybe he sneered. It could have been either with a face like his. When he spoke again, though, there was no mistaking his hatred. "Kill Prospero," he growled. "And burn every one of his books."

*I*n a woodland glade nearby, another plot was unfolding – the murder of King Alonso by his brother, Sebastian. The evil Antonio was urging Sebastian on.

"Strike now," hissed Antonio, "while he's sound asleep."

"Shall I do it?"

"Why not?" Antonio purred. "Didn't we see his son, Ferdinand, swept overboard? And doesn't Claribel, his other heir, live too far away to interfere? Already I can imagine you wearing his royal robes!"

"Just as you wear your brother's?"

"Well, you've got to admit they suit me. Be quick, now. You'll never get a better chance."

Warily, Sebastian eyed the two sleeping men. There they lay, under the trees, sprawled and defenceless. King Alonso was worn out with grief for the son he'd lost and kind Gonzalo was exhausted from trying to comfort him. Yes, Sebastian would never get a better chance...

But something made him hesitate. Perhaps it was the strangeness of where they were. Why was the grass so green here and the air so sweet? And why were their clothes so fresh when they had been salty and sea-stained? And that music really was haunting...

Sebastian shrugged it all off. "You're right, Antonio," he snapped. "Let's kill them!"

Both men drew their swords.

Suddenly, in Gonzalo's ear, the music grew louder:

"While you here do snoring lie,
Open-eyed conspiracy
His time doth take.
If of life you keep a care,
Shake off slumber and beware.
Awake, awake!"

Ariel had arrived.

At once, Gonzalo stirred himself. "Swords, sirs?" he exclaimed when he saw them.

"Are we under attack?" yawned the king.

Gonzalo listened carefully to the excuses that Antonio and Sebastian made, his eyes never leaving them. As he rose to his feet, Gonzalo drew his own sword. "Perhaps, from now on, we should all be on our guard," he said drily.

But the moment for murder had passed.

*A*fter this, Ariel enjoyed himself more than ever. Still following Prospero's instructions, he led the shipwrecked travellers all over the island, playing terrifying tricks on them. And through their confusion and misery they could each see their own weaknesses more clearly.

For the royals, Ariel laid out the most lavish and magical picnic they'd ever tasted. Or would have tasted, that is. Before they could swallow a mouthful, Ariel had swooped out of the sky disguised as a harpy – a monster, half-bird and half-woman – cackling crazily about the wrong they'd done Prospero.

"*Prospero?*" they gasped. "All this is Prospero's doing?"

Only Gonzalo smiled at the name.

Next, Ariel returned to Stephano, Trinculo and Caliban – luring them through thorn bushes and foul-smelling puddles. He even provided a complete change of clothes. But once they were clean and dry again, Ariel conjured a pack of hunting dogs to chase them back to the thorns and puddles.

They were far too distracted even to think about killing Prospero.

*B*ut what about Prince Ferdinand?

His fate was rather different. No matter what task Prospero set him, Ferdinand performed it cheerfully – and he was clearly as much in love with Miranda as she was with him. Eventually, even the magician himself was convinced.

"You've earned my trust," Prospero told Ferdinand. "So let me give you my blessing, young man."

"Your blessing, father?" asked Miranda.

Ferdinand understood at once. "Sir, you mean—"

"That the two of you may be married, yes. But be patient a little longer, my dears. My work isn't over yet. Soon I shall bring these spells of mine to an end – the last in a lifetime of magic. No, don't be upset. Like a dream at daybreak, everything on Earth will fade eventually."

"Father?" asked Miranda in alarm.

But Prospero, deep in thought, had already turned away.

The magic had been a little rough, perhaps...
but it seemed to have worked. By the time Ariel
had rounded up Prospero's prisoners in a grove
of trees that held them spellbound, they knew
there was no escape.

Ariel hurried to make his report. "All present, Master," he declared. "They're all in such a state, thanks to your magic, that even I might pity them."

"You, imp?" asked Prospero.

"Well, I would... if I were human like you."

"Now that they're sorry, my task is over. Fetch them here to me – and bring the ship and its crew to a harbour close by. Spirit, you've almost won the freedom I promised you."

"Thanks, Master!"

In a trice, Ariel had gone.

Ariel's master had vanished, too, in a way. For Prospero, the magician, was no more. He'd slipped out of his magic cloak, snapped his magic wand in two and hurled his spellbooks into the sea. Instead, from now onwards, he wore the hat and sword of a duke – the rightful Duke of Milan.

$\mathcal{A}$s soon as they saw him, the royal party was stunned.

"Is this the man I betrayed?" asked King Alonso in despair.

"Are you really Prospero?" Gonzalo gasped. "Or another of these island visions?"

"I'm just as real as you are, old friend," Prospero replied. "And just as honourable, too, I hope. I know exactly who's guilty here."

He paused a moment.

Antonio and Sebastian looked shame-faced.
Were they genuinely repentant, or simply unhappy
that they'd been found out? Whichever it was,
they seemed to shrivel under Prospero's gaze.

"Those who stole my dukedom," he said, "I
now forgive freely and fully... even as I take back
my title and everything that goes with it."

"I thank you humbly," said King Alonso. "Considering how badly I treated you, sir, I don't deserve such mercy. If I seem less grateful than I should be, I beg your pardon for my distress. Today, you see, I lost my only son in that terrible storm."

"And I, sir, lost my only daughter," said Prospero. "You did?"

"Willingly," replied Prospero. "For thanks to our children, Alonso, your land and mine will be at peace again."

He pulled aside a curtain at the back of the cave. And there, in a world of their own, sat Ferdinand and Miranda, playing chess.

It was a moment as magical and powerful, perhaps, as any conjured from a spellbook.

Later, with everyone back on board ship, Alonso put to sea again. Prospero and Miranda sailed with them as guests of honour. After all, one had a dukedom to reclaim and the other had to prepare for a royal wedding. They left behind the island that had been their home for so long.

*A*nd faithful Ariel got his wish. These days, being free to choose for himself, he's likely to end up anywhere, singing:

> "*Where the bee sucks, there suck I;*
> *In a cowslip's bell I lie:*
> *There I couch when owls do cry.*
> *On the bat's back I do fly*
> *After summer merrily...*"

Suddenly the island was empty... or almost. Just as he had always wanted, Caliban is the owner now. As far as anyone knows, he spends his time there all alone, as miserable as ever. Maybe even he misses Ariel's music.

The Shakespeare Collection

Look out for these other titles in the Shakespeare Collection:

Hamlet Retold by Anthony Masters
When Hamlet's mother remarries shortly after his father's death he's suspicious. And when his father's ghost tells him that he was murdered by the queen's new husband, Hamlet swears to take his revenge. But how...?

Twelfth Night Retold by Jan Dean
Love is in the air... The duke is in love with Olivia, who's in love with his manservant, Cesario. The trouble is, Cesario is really a woman in disguise – and she's in love with the duke! Will the course of true love ever run smooth?

Antony and Cleopatra Retold by Kathy Elgin
Antony was once the bravest general of the Roman Empire... That is, until he fell in love with Cleopatra. With war in the air and the Empire falling apart, can Antony put everything right, or will it all end in disaster?

You can buy all these books from your local bookseller, or order them direct from the publisher. For more information about The Shakespeare Collection, write to: *The Sales Department, Hodder Children's Books, a division of Hodder Headline Limited, 338 Euston Road, London NW1 3BH.*